IN THE NAME OF

ALLAH

THE ALL-COMPASSIONATE, ALL-MERCIFUL

DUTIFULNESS TO PARENTS

- Title: DUTIFULNESS TO PARENTS
- Author: Nidhām Sakkajh
- English Edition 1 (1999)
- English Edition 2 (2005)
- Layout: IIPH, Riyadh, Saudi Arabia
- Filming & Cover Designing: Samo Press Group

DUTIFULNESS TO PARENTS

In the Light of the Holy Qur'an and the Authentic Sunnah

برّ الوالدين على ضوء الكتاب و السنّة

by

Nidhām Sakkajh

Translated by

Īmān Zakariya Abu Ghāzi

INTERNATIONAL ISLAMIC PUBLISHING HOUSE

King Fahd National Library Cataloging-in-Publication Data

Sakkijha, Nidhâm

Dutifulness to parents in the light of the Holy Qur'an and the Authentic Sunnah. / Nidhām Sakkijha .- Riyadh, 2005

...p ; 20 cm

1- Parents - Attitudes I-Title

ISBN: **9960-850-52-8**

212.5 dc 1424/4713

Legal Deposit no. **1424/4713**
ISBN: **9960-850-52-8**

International Islamic Publishing House (IIPH)
P.O.Box 55195 Riyadh 11534, Saudi Arabia
Tel: 966 1 4650818 – 4647213 – Fax: 4633489
E-Mail: iiph@iiph.com.sa – www.iiph.com.sa

---

*Please take part in this noble work by conveying your comments to **IIPH through** e-mail, fax or postal-mail address.*

List of Contents

Publisher's Note 07

In the Name of Allah... 09

Introduction 11

Dutifulness to Parents 19

The Qur'an's commandment regarding parents 19

Dutifulness to parents is one of the Prophet's noted characteristics 24

Dutifulness to parents follows immediately after worshipping Allah 29

Dutifulness to parents admits one to Paradise, whereas undutifulness leads to Hell-fire 31

Allah's Pleasure comes through parents' pleasure and His Anger comes through their anger 38

Undutifulness to parents is forbidden 39

Undutifulness to parents is a grave sin 42

Dutifulness to parents precedes fighting in Allah's cause (Jihad) 44

Leaving Jihad for (the purpose of) serving parents; because Paradise is underneath their feet 44

Dutifulness to parents is of the righteous deeds one can invoke Allah with 48

Parents' pleasure precedes the wife's pleasure 50

Dutifulness to the mother precedes dutifulness to father 51

Parents' invocations are answerable 53

Kindness to parents 54

The parents' favour to their children is great 60

Abusing and cursing one's parents is a great sin 60

The son is of his father's earnings 60

Dutifulness to parents after their death 64

Parents should raise their children well to make them righteous 66

Conclusion 71

Symbols used in this book 74

Glossary 75

Transliteration Chart 77

Publisher's Note

The All-Mighty Allah, has commanded people to be kind and loyal to parents. This commandment is an obligation in all revealed religions. Islam has further emphasized obedience to parents. Is it not the right of the parents, who take the child with care from childhood to adulthood, that their goodness be rewarded? One should respect the parents, love them and care for them when they grow old and need kindness. In other words, he should help them in the same way a child needs help. Learning their rights and consciously seeking their pleasure is not only a divine order, but also an act of worship and a human attribute.

The author of this book has featured out all the aspects of this subject and has pointed out all the adverse effects emanating from the lack of dutifulness to parents. As a matter of fact, dutifulness to parents is the source of all happiness because it pleases Allah (سبحانه وتعالى).

I pray to Allah (سبحانه وتعالى) that our brothers and sisters in the English speaking world benefit from this book and may Allah reward all of us and may His peace and blessings be upon Muhammad, his family, his Companions and the nations following him till the end of this world.

Muhammad 'Abdul-Muḥsin Al Tuwaijri

International Islamic Publishing House

Riyadh, Saudi Arabia AH 1425 / CE 2004

بِسْمِ ٱللَّهِ ٱلرَّحْمَٰنِ ٱلرَّحِيمِ

﴿ٱلْحَمْدُ لِلَّهِ رَبِّ ٱلْعَٰلَمِينَ ۝٢ ٱلرَّحْمَٰنِ
ٱلرَّحِيمِ ۝٣ مَٰلِكِ يَوْمِ ٱلدِّينِ ۝٤ إِيَّاكَ نَعْبُدُ
وَإِيَّاكَ نَسْتَعِينُ ۝٥ ٱهْدِنَا ٱلصِّرَٰطَ ٱلْمُسْتَقِيمَ ۝٦
صِرَٰطَ ٱلَّذِينَ أَنْعَمْتَ عَلَيْهِمْ غَيْرِ ٱلْمَغْضُوبِ عَلَيْهِمْ
وَلَا ٱلضَّآلِّينَ ۝٧﴾ (سورة الفاتحة: ٢-٧)

In the Name of Allah,
the All-Beneficent, All-Merciful

﴾All the praise and thanks be to Allah, the Lord of the *'Ālamīn* [mankind, jinn, and all that exists]. The Most Beneficent, the Most Merciful. The only owner [and the only Ruling Judge] of the Day of Recompense [i.e., the Day of Resurrection]. You [Alone] we worship, and you [Alone] we ask for help [for each and every thing]. Guide us to the straightway. The way of those on whom you have bestowed your Grace, not [the way] of those who earned your Anger, nor of those who went astray.﴿

(Qur'an 1: 2-7)

﴿الٓمٓ ۝١ ذَٰلِكَ ٱلْكِتَٰبُ لَا رَيْبَ فِيهِ هُدًى لِّلْمُتَّقِينَ ۝٢
ٱلَّذِينَ يُؤْمِنُونَ بِٱلْغَيْبِ وَيُقِيمُونَ ٱلصَّلَوٰةَ وَمِمَّا رَزَقْنَٰهُمْ
يُنفِقُونَ ۝٣ وَٱلَّذِينَ يُؤْمِنُونَ بِمَآ أُنزِلَ إِلَيْكَ وَمَآ أُنزِلَ مِن
قَبْلِكَ وَبِٱلْءَاخِرَةِ هُمْ يُوقِنُونَ ۝٤ أُو۟لَٰٓئِكَ عَلَىٰ هُدًى مِّن رَّبِّهِمْ
وَأُو۟لَٰٓئِكَ هُمُ ٱلْمُفْلِحُونَ ۝٥﴾ (سورة البقرة: ١-٥)

﴿*Alif-Lām-Mīm*. [These letters are one of the miracles of the Qur'an and none but Allah (Alone) knows their meanings.] This is the Book [the Qur'an], whereof there is no doubt, and guidance to those who are *al-Muttaqūn* [the pious, righteous persons who fear Allah much (abstain from all kinds of sins and evil deeds which He has forbidden) and love Allah much (perform all kinds of good deeds which He has ordained)]. Who believe in the *Ghayb* (the invisible) [i.e., Allah, His angels, His Messengers, His Books, Day of Resurrection, Divine Ordainment... etc] and perform *Ṣalāh* [Prayers] and spend out of what we have provided for them [i.e., give Zakah [poor due], spend on themselves, their parents, their children, their wives, etc., and also give charity to the poor and in Allah's Cause — Jihad (Holy War), etc.,]. And who believe in [the Qur'an and the Sunnah] what has been sent down to you [Muhammad] and in the *Taurāt* [Torah] and the *Injīl* [Gospel], etc., which were sent down before you, and believe with certainty in the Hereafter. [Resurrection, recompense of their good and bad deeds, Paradise and Hell, etc.,] They are on [true] guidance from their Lord [Allah], and they are successful.﴿

(Qur'an 2: 1-5)

﴿وَوَصَّيْنَا ٱلْإِنسَٰنَ بِوَٰلِدَيْهِ حَمَلَتْهُ أُمُّهُۥ وَهْنًا عَلَىٰ وَهْنٍ وَفِصَٰلُهُۥ فِى عَامَيْنِ أَنِ ٱشْكُرْ لِى وَلِوَٰلِدَيْكَ إِلَىَّ ٱلْمَصِيرُ ﴿١٤﴾ وَإِن جَٰهَدَاكَ عَلَىٰٓ أَن تُشْرِكَ بِى مَا لَيْسَ لَكَ بِهِۦ عِلْمٌ فَلَا تُطِعْهُمَا ۖ وَصَاحِبْهُمَا فِى ٱلدُّنْيَا مَعْرُوفًا ۖ وَٱتَّبِعْ سَبِيلَ مَنْ أَنَابَ إِلَىَّ ۚ ثُمَّ إِلَىَّ مَرْجِعُكُمْ فَأُنَبِّئُكُم بِمَا كُنتُمْ تَعْمَلُونَ ﴿١٥﴾﴾

(سورة لقمان: ١٤-١٥)

﴾And We have enjoined on man [to be dutiful and good] to his parents, His mother bore him in weakness and hardship upon weakness and hardship, and his weaning is in two years — give thanks to Me and to your parents. Unto Me is the final destination. But if they [both] strive with you to make you join in worship with Me others that of which you have no knowledge, then obey them not; but behave with them in the world kindly and follow the path of him who turns to Me in repentance and in obedience. Then to Me will be your return, and I shall tell you what you used to do.﴿ *(Qur'an 31: 14-15)*

Introduction

All praise is due to Allah (ﷻ). We thank Him, seek His help and forgiveness, and we seek refuge with Allah from the evils of ourselves and our bad deeds. Whosoever has been guided by Allah, none can misguide him. And whosoever has been misguided by Allah, none can guide him. I bear witness that there is no true deity but Allah, being Alone without any partner, and I bear witness that Muhammad (ﷺ) 'Blessings and Peace be upon him,' is His slave and Messenger.

Allah (ﷻ) says:

﴿يَٰٓأَيُّهَا ٱلَّذِينَ ءَامَنُوا۟ ٱتَّقُوا۟ ٱللَّهَ حَقَّ تُقَاتِهِۦ وَلَا تَمُوتُنَّ إِلَّا وَأَنتُم مُّسْلِمُونَ ﴿١٠٢﴾﴾

(سورة آل عِمرَان: ١٠٢)

﴾O' you who believe! Fear Allah [by doing all that He has ordered and by abstaining from all that He has forbidden] as He should be feared. [Obey Him, be thankful to Him, and remember Him always], and die not except as Muslims [with complete submission to Allah].﴿ *(Qur'an 3: 102)*

He, (ﷻ) also says:

﴿ يَٰٓأَيُّهَا ٱلنَّاسُ ٱتَّقُواْ رَبَّكُمُ ٱلَّذِى خَلَقَكُم مِّن نَّفْسٍ وَٰحِدَةٍ وَخَلَقَ مِنْهَا زَوْجَهَا وَبَثَّ مِنْهُمَا رِجَالًا كَثِيرًا وَنِسَآءً ۚ وَٱتَّقُواْ ٱللَّهَ ٱلَّذِى تَسَآءَلُونَ بِهِۦ وَٱلْأَرْحَامَ ۚ إِنَّ ٱللَّهَ كَانَ عَلَيْكُمْ رَقِيبًا ﴿١﴾ ﴾ (سورة النساء: ١)

﴾O' mankind! Be dutiful to your Lord, Who created you from a single person [Ādam], and from him [Ādam] He created his wife [Ḥawwā' (Eve)], and from them both He created many men and women, and fear Allah through Whom you demand [your mutual rights], and [do not cut the relations of] the wombs [kinship]. Surely, Allah is Ever All-Watcher over you.﴿ *(Qur'an 4: 1)*

Yet in another place, the All-High says:

﴿ يَٰٓأَيُّهَا ٱلَّذِينَ ءَامَنُواْ ٱتَّقُواْ ٱللَّهَ وَقُولُواْ قَوْلًا سَدِيدًا ﴿٧٠﴾ يُصْلِحْ لَكُمْ أَعْمَٰلَكُمْ وَيَغْفِرْ لَكُمْ ذُنُوبَكُمْ ۗ وَمَن يُطِعِ ٱللَّهَ وَرَسُولَهُۥ فَقَدْ فَازَ فَوْزًا عَظِيمًا ﴿٧١﴾ ﴾ (سورة الأحزاب: ٧٠-٧١)

﴾O' you who believe! Be dutiful to your Lord and fear Him, and speak [always] the truth. He will direct you to do righteous good deeds and will forgive your sins. And whosoever obeys Allah and His Messenger, has indeed achieved a great achievement [i.e. will be saved from the Hell-fire and made to enter Paradise].﴿ *(Qur'an 33: 70-71)*

Verily, the best speech is that of the Book of Allah, and the best guidance is the Prophet's guidance, and the worst (most evil) of things are the innovations in religion, and every innovation is an act of misguidance.

I performed the Friday prayer on Rabīʻ al-Awwal 16th, (the third month of the Hijrah Calendar / 1403 A.H. in Ṣalāḥ ad-Dīn mosque in Ammān, Jordan. The *Khaṭīb* (the one who delivers the sermon) was my brother and tutor Abu Mālik, Muhammad Ibrāhīm Shaqrah, 'may Allah bless him,' and make his works of great benefit to others. His sermon reminded those praying in the mosque of the necessity of precisely following the orders of Allah's Book, the Qur'an and His Messenger's Sunnah. While doing so, he narrated one of the Prophet's hadiths (sayings), from Anas ibn Mālik (رضي الله عنه) 'may Allah be pleased with him': "The Prophet (ﷺ) ascended one of the pulpit stairs and said; *Āmīn*, and ascended the second one and said; *Āmīn* and ascended the third one and said, *Āmīn*. Then he (ﷺ) sat on the pulpit." His Companions asked: "Why did you say *Āmīn*?" He (ﷺ) said:

> "Gibrīl [(Gabriel) (عليه السلام) 'May Peace be upon him],' came to me and said: 'May his nose be covered with dust,[1] he before whom I [Muhammad] was

[1] This is an Arabic expression to indicate that the addressee is losing something valuable. (Translator)

> mentioned and he did not pray for Allah's blessings on me.' Then I said: '*Āmīn.*' Then he (Gibrīl) said: 'May his nose be covered with dust, he whose parents lived till he attained the age of puberty and was not admitted to paradise (after his death because of his ill behaviour towards them). I said: '*Āmīn.*' Then he (Gibrīl) said: 'May his nose be covered with dust, he who witnessed (the month of) Ramaḍān and was (or his sins were) not forgiven (on account of his evil actions in this sacred month). Then I said: '*Āmīn*'.' "[2]

This Prophetic hadith touched the bottom of my heart, and induced me to write this booklet, gathering the Qur'anic verses and the authentic Prophetic sayings dealing with the issue of *Dutifulness to Parents*, at a time when many Muslims (neglected and) moved away from taking care of their fathers and mothers, and when their religious spirit has so fainted, that they did not (and do not) give their parents their rights which Allah (ﷻ) enjoined on them.

I, therefore, made up my mind, putting my trust in Allah, the All-Mighty, (to give me the power to write the book) and started reading Allah's Book (the Qur'an), taking heed and examining carefully the verses, so that I could find

---

[2] *Faḍl aṣ-Ṣalāt 'ala an-Nabi*, Pp. 30-33, by Ismaīl ibn Isḥāq. Shaykh Nāsiruddīn al-Albāni has collected and authenticated the hadith with a number of chain of narrators.

every verse that pertains to the issue of this book. Then I searched for the authentic hadiths in the *Sunan* (hadith books) and cited only those that were authenticated by the early and contemporary scholars of hadith.

While reading about the subject and studying it, my reverend teacher Shaykh Muhammad Nāṣirud-Dīn al-Albāni, informed me that there was a published paper about *Dutifulness to Parents* by 'Abdur Ra'ūf al-Ḥinnāwi. I managed to get it from one of my Muslim brothers, I read it, scrutinized it and gained a lot of benefit from it. However, the paper's way of discussing the subject was totally different from the track I adopted. It contained a lot of weak hadiths and long stories about people whose origin could not be authenticated. Whereas I in my treatise, confined myself only to the Qur'anic verses, explaining their difficult meanings, depending on Ibn Kathīr's interpretation of the Glorious Qur'an and the authentic Hadiths.

I am indeed indebted to my reverend teacher Shaykh Muhammad Nāṣirud-Dīn al-Albāni, who generously granted me the manuscript of his book *Ṣaḥīḥ at-Targhīb wat Tarhīb*, of which the first volume has been recently published. I ask Allah, the Almighty, to pave the way for the remaining volumes of the book to see the light of the day. This book greatly benefitted in knowing the authentic hadiths related to my subject.

I am also grateful to brother Shaykh 'Awny ash-Sharīf, who offered me an index for *Ṣaḥīḥ al-Jāmi'*, arranged alphabetically according to the titles of subjects the book contains. It made easier for me to find the authentic hadiths related to my subject. I also offer my gratitude to all those who offered me their help with advice, and guided me. I invoke Allah (ﷻ) to make this paper beneficial to all Muslims, benefit me after death. May it become for His sake only and the All-High, grant me its reward. May Allah also make me one of those who are dutiful to their parents.

Allah (ﷻ) says:

﴿يَوْمَ لَا يَنفَعُ مَالٌ وَلَا بَنُونَ ﴿٨٨﴾ إِلَّا مَنْ أَتَى ٱللَّهَ بِقَلْبٍ سَلِيمٍ ﴿٨٩﴾﴾

(سورة الشُّعَرَاء: ٨٨-٨٩)

﴾The Day whereon neither wealth nor sons will avail. Except him who approaches Allah with a clean heart [clean from *shirk* (polytheism) and *nifāq* (hypocrisy)].﴿ *(Qur'an 26 : 88-89)*

Nidhām Sakkijha

Dutifulness to Parents

The Qur'an's commandment regarding parents

Allah (سبحانه وتعالى) says:

﴿ وَقَضَىٰ رَبُّكَ أَلَّا تَعْبُدُوٓا۟ إِلَّآ إِيَّاهُ وَبِٱلْوَٰلِدَيْنِ إِحْسَٰنًا ۚ إِمَّا
يَبْلُغَنَّ عِندَكَ ٱلْكِبَرَ أَحَدُهُمَآ أَوْ كِلَاهُمَا فَلَا تَقُل لَّهُمَآ
أُفٍّ وَلَا تَنْهَرْهُمَا وَقُل لَّهُمَا قَوْلًا كَرِيمًا ﴿٢٣﴾ وَٱخْفِضْ
لَهُمَا جَنَاحَ ٱلذُّلِّ مِنَ ٱلرَّحْمَةِ وَقُل رَّبِّ ٱرْحَمْهُمَا كَمَا رَبَّيَانِى
صَغِيرًا ﴿٢٤﴾ رَّبُّكُمْ أَعْلَمُ بِمَا فِى نُفُوسِكُمْ ۚ إِن تَكُونُوا۟ صَٰلِحِينَ
فَإِنَّهُۥ كَانَ لِلْأَوَّٰبِينَ غَفُورًا ﴿٢٥﴾ ﴾ (سورة الإسراء: ٢٣-٢٥)

﴿And your Lord [Allah] has decreed that you worship none but Him. And that you be dutiful to your parents. If one of them or both of them attain old age while with you, say not to them '*uff*' [disapproval or irritation], nor shout at them, but address them in terms of honour. And lower unto them the wing of submission and humility through mercy, and say: 'My [Lord]! Bestow on them your

Mercy as they did bring me up when I was small.' Your Lord knows best what is in your inner-selves. If you are righteous, then, verily, He is Ever Oft-Forgiving to those who turn unto Him again and again in obedience and in repentance.﴿

(Qur'an 17: 23-25)

﴿وَوَصَّيۡنَا ٱلۡإِنسَٰنَ بِوَٰلِدَيۡهِ حَمَلَتۡهُ أُمُّهُۥ وَهۡنًا عَلَىٰ وَهۡنٖ
وَفِصَٰلُهُۥ فِي عَامَيۡنِ أَنِ ٱشۡكُرۡ لِي وَلِوَٰلِدَيۡكَ إِلَيَّ ٱلۡمَصِيرُ
١٤ وَإِن جَٰهَدَاكَ عَلَىٰٓ أَن تُشۡرِكَ بِي مَا لَيۡسَ لَكَ بِهِۦ عِلۡمٞ فَلَا
تُطِعۡهُمَاۖ وَصَاحِبۡهُمَا فِي ٱلدُّنۡيَا مَعۡرُوفٗاۖ وَٱتَّبِعۡ سَبِيلَ مَنۡ أَنَابَ
إِلَيَّۚ ثُمَّ إِلَيَّ مَرۡجِعُكُمۡ فَأُنَبِّئُكُم بِمَا كُنتُمۡ تَعۡمَلُونَ ١٥﴾

(سورة لقمان: ١٤-١٥)

﴾And We have enjoined on man [to be dutiful and good] to his parents. His mother bore him in weakness and hardship upon weakness and hardship, and his weaning is in two years — give thanks to Me and to your parents. Unto Me is the final destination. But if they [both] strive with you to make you join in worship with Me others that of which you have no knowledge, then obey them not, but behave with them in the world kindly, and follow the path of him who turns to Me in repentance and in obedience. Then to Me will be your return, and I shall tell you what you used to do.﴿ *(Qur'an 31: 14-15)*

﴿وَوَصَّيۡنَا ٱلۡإِنسَٰنَ بِوَٰلِدَيۡهِ حُسۡنٗاۖ وَإِن جَٰهَدَاكَ لِتُشۡرِكَ بِي مَا
لَيۡسَ لَكَ بِهِۦ عِلۡمٞ فَلَا تُطِعۡهُمَآۚ إِلَيَّ مَرۡجِعُكُمۡ فَأُنَبِّئُكُم بِمَا
كُنتُمۡ تَعۡمَلُونَ ٨﴾ (سورة العنكبوت : ٨)

﴿And We have enjoined on man to be good and dutiful to his parents; but if they strive to make you join with Me [in worship] any thing [as a partner] of which you have no knowledge, then obey them not. Unto Me is your return, and I shall tell you what you used to do.﴾ *(Qur'an 29: 8)*

﴿وَوَصَّيۡنَا ٱلۡإِنسَٰنَ بِوَٰلِدَيۡهِ إِحۡسَٰنًاۖ حَمَلَتۡهُ أُمُّهُۥ كُرۡهٗا وَوَضَعَتۡهُ
كُرۡهٗاۖ وَحَمۡلُهُۥ وَفِصَٰلُهُۥ ثَلَٰثُونَ شَهۡرًاۚ حَتَّىٰٓ إِذَا بَلَغَ أَشُدَّهُۥ وَبَلَغَ
أَرۡبَعِينَ سَنَةٗ قَالَ رَبِّ أَوۡزِعۡنِيٓ أَنۡ أَشۡكُرَ نِعۡمَتَكَ ٱلَّتِيٓ أَنۡعَمۡتَ
عَلَيَّ وَعَلَىٰ وَٰلِدَيَّ وَأَنۡ أَعۡمَلَ صَٰلِحٗا تَرۡضَىٰهُ وَأَصۡلِحۡ لِي فِي
ذُرِّيَّتِيٓۖ إِنِّي تُبۡتُ إِلَيۡكَ وَإِنِّي مِنَ ٱلۡمُسۡلِمِينَ ١٥ أُوْلَٰٓئِكَ ٱلَّذِينَ
نَتَقَبَّلُ عَنۡهُمۡ أَحۡسَنَ مَا عَمِلُواْ وَنَتَجَاوَزُ عَن سَيِّـَٔاتِهِمۡ فِيٓ أَصۡحَٰبِ
ٱلۡجَنَّةِۖ وَعۡدَ ٱلصِّدۡقِ ٱلَّذِي كَانُواْ يُوعَدُونَ ١٦ وَٱلَّذِي قَالَ
لِوَٰلِدَيۡهِ أُفّٖ لَّكُمَآ أَتَعِدَانِنِيٓ أَنۡ أُخۡرَجَ وَقَدۡ خَلَتِ ٱلۡقُرُونُ مِن
قَبۡلِي وَهُمَا يَسۡتَغِيثَانِ ٱللَّهَ وَيۡلَكَ ءَامِنۡ إِنَّ وَعۡدَ ٱللَّهِ حَقّٞ فَيَقُولُ مَا
هَٰذَآ إِلَّآ أَسَٰطِيرُ ٱلۡأَوَّلِينَ ١٧ أُوْلَٰٓئِكَ ٱلَّذِينَ حَقَّ عَلَيۡهِمُ
ٱلۡقَوۡلُ فِيٓ أُمَمٖ قَدۡ خَلَتۡ مِن قَبۡلِهِم مِّنَ ٱلۡجِنِّ وَٱلۡإِنسِۖ إِنَّهُمۡ كَانُواْ
خَٰسِرِينَ ١٨ وَلِكُلّٖ دَرَجَٰتٞ مِّمَّا عَمِلُواْۖ وَلِيُوَفِّيَهُمۡ أَعۡمَٰلَهُمۡ وَهُمۡ لَا

يُظْلَمُونَ ﴿١٩﴾ وَيَوْمَ يُعْرَضُ ٱلَّذِينَ كَفَرُوا۟ عَلَى ٱلنَّارِ أَذْهَبْتُمْ طَيِّبَٰتِكُمْ فِى
حَيَاتِكُمُ ٱلدُّنْيَا وَٱسْتَمْتَعْتُم بِهَا فَٱلْيَوْمَ تُجْزَوْنَ عَذَابَ ٱلْهُونِ بِمَا
كُنتُمْ تَسْتَكْبِرُونَ فِى ٱلْأَرْضِ بِغَيْرِ ٱلْحَقِّ وَبِمَا كُنتُمْ تَفْسُقُونَ ﴿٢٠﴾﴾

(سورة الأحقاف: ١٥-٢٠)

﴿And We enjoined on man to be dutiful and kind to his parents. His mother bears him with hardship. And she brings him forth with hardship, and the bearing of him, and the weaning of him is thirty months, till when he attains full strength and reaches forty years, he says: 'My Lord! Grant me the power and ability that I may be grateful for Your Favour, which You have bestow-ed upon me, and upon my parents, and that I may do righteous, good deeds, so as to please You, and, my Lord make righteous for me my off-spring. Truly, I have turned to You in repentance, and truly, I am one of the Muslims [submitting to Your Will].' They are those from whom We shall accept the best of their deeds and overlook their evil deeds. [They shall be] among the dwellers of Paradise — a promise of truth, which they have been promised. But he who says to his parents: 'Fie upon you both! Do you hold out the promise to me that I shall be raised up [again] when generations before me have passed away [without rising]?' While they [father and mother] invoke Allah for help [and rebuke their son]: 'Woe to you! Believe! Verily, the promise of Allah is true.' But he says: 'This is nothing but false tales of the ancient.' They are those against whom the Word [of torment] is justified among the previous [nations or] generations of jinn and mankind that have passed away. Verily, they are ever the losers. And for all, there will be degrees according to that which they did, that He [Allah] may recompense them in full for their deeds. And they will not be wronged. On the Day when those who disbelieve [in the Oneness of Allah — Islamic Monotheism] will be exposed to the Fire [it will be said]: 'You received your good things in the life of the world, and you took your pleasure and abused them therein. Today you shall be recompensed with a torment of humiliation, because you were arrogant in the land without a right, and because you used to rebel and disobey [Allah].﴿

(Qur'an 46: 15-20)

﴾يَسْـَٔلُونَكَ مَاذَا يُنفِقُونَ ۖ قُلْ مَآ أَنفَقْتُم مِّنْ خَيْرٍ فَلِلْوَٰلِدَيْنِ وَٱلْأَقْرَبِينَ وَٱلْيَتَـٰمَىٰ وَٱلْمَسَـٰكِينِ وَٱبْنِ ٱلسَّبِيلِ ۗ وَمَا تَفْعَلُوا۟ مِنْ خَيْرٍ فَإِنَّ ٱللَّهَ بِهِۦ عَلِيمٌ ﴿٢١٥﴾﴿

(سورة البقرة: ٢١٥)

﴾They ask you [O' Muḥammad] what they should spend. Say: 'Whatever you spend of good must be for parents and kindred and orphans and *al-masākīn* [the poor] and the wayfarers, and

> whatever you do of good deeds, truly, Allah knows it well.﴿ *(Qur'an 2: 215)*

In the previous verse, Allah (ﷻ), mentioned parents ahead of kindred, orphans, the poor, and the wayfarers, when talking about giving charities (and those supposed to receive them). The following hadith also supports the previous point. The Prophet (ﷺ) said:

> "Whatever you spend of good must be for your mother, your father, your sister, your brother, then the lower, then the lowest (regarding kinship)."

This hadith will be (fully) stated in the section regarding the precedence of the mother's right to the father's.

Dutifulness to parents is one of the Prophets' noted characteristics

1. Allah, the Exalted, All-Glorious, says — talking about 'Eesa ibn Maryam (عليه السلام) 'peace be upon him' (Jesus, son of Mary):

﴾قَالَ إِنِّي عَبْدُ ٱللَّهِ ءَاتَىٰنِيَ ٱلْكِتَٰبَ وَجَعَلَنِي نَبِيًّا ﴿٣٠﴾ وَجَعَلَنِي
مُبَارَكًا أَيْنَ مَا كُنتُ وَأَوْصَٰنِي بِٱلصَّلَوٰةِ وَٱلزَّكَوٰةِ مَا دُمْتُ
حَيًّا ﴿٣١﴾ وَبَرًّۢا بِوَٰلِدَتِي وَلَمْ يَجْعَلْنِي جَبَّارًا شَقِيًّا ﴿٣٢﴾ وَٱلسَّلَٰمُ
عَلَيَّ يَوْمَ وُلِدتُّ وَيَوْمَ أَمُوتُ وَيَوْمَ أُبْعَثُ حَيًّا ﴿٣٣﴾ ذَٰلِكَ

﴿عِيسَى ٱبْنُ مَرْيَمَ ۚ قَوْلَ ٱلْحَقِّ ٱلَّذِى فِيهِ يَمْتَرُونَ ﴿٣٤﴾﴾

(سورة مَريَم : ٣٠-٣٤)

﴾He [Eesā (Jesus)] said: 'Verily, I am a slave of Allah, He has given me the Scripture and made me a Prophet. And He has made me blessed wheresoever I might be, and has enjoined on me *Ṣalāh* [prayer], and Zakah [poor due], as long as I live.' 'And dutiful to my mother, but made me not arrogant, unblest. And *Salām* [peace] be upon me the day I was born, the day I die and the day I shall be raised alive!' Such is Eesā, son of Maryam [Mary], [It is] a statement of truth, about which they doubt [or dispute].﴿ *(Qur'an 19: 30-34)*

2. Allah (سبحانه وتعالى) also says — talking about — Prophet Ibrahīm (Abraham) (عليه السلام),

﴿رَبِّ ٱجْعَلْنِى مُقِيمَ ٱلصَّلَوٰةِ وَمِن ذُرِّيَّتِى ۚ رَبَّنَا وَتَقَبَّلْ دُعَآءِ ﴿٤٠﴾ رَبَّنَا ٱغْفِرْ لِى وَلِوَٰلِدَىَّ وَلِلْمُؤْمِنِينَ يَوْمَ يَقُومُ ٱلْحِسَابُ ﴿٤١﴾﴾

(سورة إبراهيم : ٤٠-٤١)

﴾'O' my Lord! Make me an establisher of prayers, and [many] from my offspring. O' our Lord, and accept our supplications. Our God, Forgive me and my parents, and [all] the believers on the Day when the reckoning will be established.'﴿

(Qur'an 14: 40-41)

3. He (سبحانه وتعالى) says:

﴿رَبِّ هَبْ لِي حُكْمًا وَأَلْحِقْنِي بِالصَّالِحِينَ ﴿٨٣﴾ وَاجْعَل لِّي
لِسَانَ صِدْقٍ فِي الْآخِرِينَ ﴿٨٤﴾ وَاجْعَلْنِي مِن وَرَثَةِ جَنَّةِ النَّعِيمِ ﴿٨٥﴾
وَاغْفِرْ لِأَبِي إِنَّهُ كَانَ مِنَ الضَّالِّينَ ﴿٨٦﴾ وَلَا تُخْزِنِي يَوْمَ يُبْعَثُونَ
﴿٨٧﴾﴾

(سورة الشُّعَرَاء: ٨٣-٨٧)

﴿My Lord! Bestow *Ḥukm* [religious knowledge, right judgement of the affairs and Prophethood] on me, and join me with the righteous. And grant me an honorable mention in later generations. And make me one of the inheritors of the Paradise of Delight. And forgive my father, verily he is of the erring. And disgrace me not on the Day when they [all the creatures] will be resurrected.﴾

(Qur'an 26: 83-87)

4. And about Prophet Sulaymān (Solomon) (عليه السلام), He (سبحانه وتعالى) says:

﴿حَتَّىٰ إِذَا أَتَوْا عَلَىٰ وَادِ النَّمْلِ قَالَتْ نَمْلَةٌ يَا أَيُّهَا النَّمْلُ ادْخُلُوا
مَسَاكِنَكُمْ لَا يَحْطِمَنَّكُمْ سُلَيْمَانُ وَجُنُودُهُ وَهُمْ لَا يَشْعُرُونَ ﴿١٨﴾
فَتَبَسَّمَ ضَاحِكًا مِّن قَوْلِهَا وَقَالَ رَبِّ أَوْزِعْنِي أَنْ أَشْكُرَ
نِعْمَتَكَ الَّتِي أَنْعَمْتَ عَلَيَّ وَعَلَىٰ وَالِدَيَّ وَأَنْ أَعْمَلَ صَالِحًا
تَرْضَاهُ وَأَدْخِلْنِي بِرَحْمَتِكَ فِي عِبَادِكَ الصَّالِحِينَ ﴿١٩﴾﴾

(سورة النَّمل: ١٨-١٩)

﴾Till they came to the valley of the ants, one of the ants said: 'O' ants! Enter your dwellings, lest Sulaymān and his soldiers should unintentionally crush you. So he [Sulaymān] smiled, amused at her speech and said: 'My Lord! Inspire me and bestow upon me the power and ability that I may be grateful for Your Favours which You have bestowed on me and on my parents, and that I may do righteous good deeds that will please You, and admit me by Your mercy among Your righteous slaves.'﴿ *(Qur'an 27: 18-19)*

5. And about Prophet Nūḥ (Noah) (عليه السلام) He (سبحانه وتعالى) says:

﴿وَقَالَ نُوحٌ رَّبِّ لَا تَذَرْ عَلَى ٱلْأَرْضِ مِنَ ٱلْكَٰفِرِينَ دَيَّارًا (٢٦) إِنَّكَ
إِن تَذَرْهُمْ يُضِلُّوا۟ عِبَادَكَ وَلَا يَلِدُوٓا۟ إِلَّا فَاجِرًا كَفَّارًا (٢٧)
رَّبِّ ٱغْفِرْ لِى وَلِوَٰلِدَىَّ وَلِمَن دَخَلَ بَيْتِىَ مُؤْمِنًا وَلِلْمُؤْمِنِينَ
وَٱلْمُؤْمِنَٰتِ وَلَا تَزِدِ ٱلظَّٰلِمِينَ إِلَّا تَبَارًۢا (٢٨)﴾

(سورة نُوح: ٢٦-٢٨)

﴾And Nūḥ [Noah] said: 'My Lord! Do not leave upon the earth from among the disbelievers an inhabitant! If You leave them, they will mislead Your slaves and will beget none but wicked disbelievers. My Lord! Forgive me, and my parents, and him who enters my home as a believer, and all the believing men and women. And do not increase wrong-doers except in destruction.'﴿ *(Qur'an 71: 26-28)*

6. And about Prophet Ismā'īl (عليه السلام), He, the Almighty, All-High, says:

﴿فَبَشَّرْنَٰهُ بِغُلَٰمٍ حَلِيمٍ ﴿١٠١﴾ فَلَمَّا بَلَغَ مَعَهُ ٱلسَّعْيَ قَالَ يَٰبُنَيَّ
إِنِّيٓ أَرَىٰ فِي ٱلْمَنَامِ أَنِّيٓ أَذْبَحُكَ فَٱنظُرْ مَاذَا تَرَىٰ ۚ قَالَ يَٰٓأَبَتِ
ٱفْعَلْ مَا تُؤْمَرُ ۖ سَتَجِدُنِيٓ إِن شَآءَ ٱللَّهُ مِنَ ٱلصَّٰبِرِينَ ﴿١٠٢﴾ فَلَمَّآ
أَسْلَمَا وَتَلَّهُۥ لِلْجَبِينِ ﴿١٠٣﴾ وَنَٰدَيْنَٰهُ أَن يَٰٓإِبْرَٰهِيمُ ﴿١٠٤﴾ قَدْ صَدَّقْتَ
ٱلرُّءْيَآ ۚ إِنَّا كَذَٰلِكَ نَجْزِي ٱلْمُحْسِنِينَ ﴿١٠٥﴾ إِنَّ هَٰذَا لَهُوَ ٱلْبَلَٰٓؤُا۟
ٱلْمُبِينُ ﴿١٠٦﴾ وَفَدَيْنَٰهُ بِذِبْحٍ عَظِيمٍ ﴿١٠٧﴾﴾

(سورة الصَّافات: ١٠١-١٠٧)

﴾So We gave him the glad tidings of a forbearing boy. And, when he reached with him [the age of] exertion — the ability to work and be of assistance — he said: 'O' my son! I have seen in a dream that I offer you in sacrifice [to Allah]. So, look what you think!' He said: 'O' my father! Do as you are commanded, *Inshā' Allāh* [if Allah so wills], you shall find me of the steadfast — *aṣ-ṣābirīn*.' Then, when they both had submitted [to the Will of Allah], and he put him [Ismā'īl] down upon his forehead We [Allah] called to him: 'O' Abraham! You have fulfilled the dream [vision]!' Verily, thus do We reward the *muḥsinīn* [good doers]. Verily, that indeed was a manifest trial, and We ransomed

him [Ismā'īl] with a great sacrifice [i.e., a ram].﴾
(Qur'an 37: 101-107)

7. And about Prophet Yaḥyā (John) (عليه السلام), He (سبحانه وتعالى) says:

﴿يَٰيَحْيَىٰ خُذِ ٱلْكِتَٰبَ بِقُوَّةٍ ۖ وَءَاتَيْنَٰهُ ٱلْحُكْمَ صَبِيًّا ﴿١٢﴾
وَحَنَانًا مِّن لَّدُنَّا وَزَكَوٰةً ۖ وَكَانَ تَقِيًّا ﴿١٣﴾ وَبَرًّۢا بِوَٰلِدَيْهِ وَلَمْ
يَكُن جَبَّارًا عَصِيًّا ﴿١٤﴾ وَسَلَٰمٌ عَلَيْهِ يَوْمَ وُلِدَ وَيَوْمَ يَمُوتُ
وَيَوْمَ يُبْعَثُ حَيًّا ﴿١٥﴾﴾ (سورة مريم: ١٢-١٥)

﴿'O' Yaḥyā [John]! Hold fast the scripture [i.e., adhere to it]. And We gave him wisdom [while yet] a boy. And affection from Us and purity, and he was fearing of Allah. And dutiful to his parents, and he was neither arrogant nor disobedient [to Allah or to his parents]. And *Salām* (peace) be on him the day he was born, the day he dies, and the day he will be raised up to life [again]!﴾
(Qur'an 19: 12-15)

Dutifulness to parents follows immediately after worshipping Allah

1. Allah (سبحانه وتعالى) says:

﴿۞ وَقَضَىٰ رَبُّكَ أَلَّا تَعْبُدُوٓا۟ إِلَّآ إِيَّاهُ وَبِٱلْوَٰلِدَيْنِ إِحْسَٰنًا ۚ ...
﴿٢٣﴾﴾ (سورة الإسراء: ٢٣)

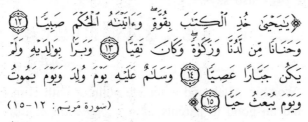

﴿And your Lord has decreed [or enjoined] that you worship none but Him. And that you be dutiful to your parents...﴾ *(Qur'an 17: 23)*

2. He (سبحانه وتعالى) also says:

﴿۞ وَٱعْبُدُوا۟ ٱللَّهَ وَلَا تُشْرِكُوا۟ بِهِۦ شَيْـًٔا ۖ وَبِٱلْوَٰلِدَيْنِ إِحْسَـٰنًا ... ﴿٣٦﴾﴾ (سورة النساء: ٣٦)

﴿Worship Allah and associate nothing with Him; and do good to parents,...﴾ *(Qur'an 4: 36)*

3. And He (سبحانه وتعالى) says:

﴿وَإِذْ أَخَذْنَا مِيثَـٰقَ بَنِىٓ إِسْرَٰٓءِيلَ لَا تَعْبُدُونَ إِلَّا ٱللَّهَ وَبِٱلْوَٰلِدَيْنِ إِحْسَانًا ... ﴿٨٣﴾﴾ (سورة البقرة: ٨٣)

﴿Remember when We took a covenant from the children of Israel, [saying]: 'Worship none but Allah [Alone] and be dutiful and good to parents,...'﴾ *(Qur'an 2: 83)*

4. And, He (سبحانه وتعالى) also says:

﴿۞ قُلْ تَعَالَوْا۟ أَتْلُ مَا حَرَّمَ رَبُّكُمْ عَلَيْكُمْ ۖ أَلَّا تُشْرِكُوا۟ بِهِۦ شَيْـًٔا ۖ وَبِٱلْوَٰلِدَيْنِ إِحْسَـٰنًا ... ﴿١٥١﴾﴾

(سورة الأنعام: ١٥١)

﴿Say [O' Muḥammad]: 'Come, I will recite what your Lord has prohibited you from: 'Do not co-worship any thing with Him; and be good and dutiful to your parents;...''﴾ *(Qur'an 6: 151)*

5. 'Abdullāh ibn Mas'ūd (ﷺ) (may Allah be pleased with him), said: "I asked Allah's Messenger about the best deed in Allah's sight." The Prophet (ﷺ) said:

> 'To perform the prayers on their appointed times.' I said: 'Then what is the next (in goodness)?' He said: 'Being dutiful to parents.'[3] I said: 'Then what is the next (in goodness)?' He said: 'To fight in Allah's cause (Jihad).' "[4]

Dutifulness to parents admits one to Paradise, whereas undutifulness leads to Hell-fire

1. Abu Hurayrah (ﷺ) narrated that the Prophet (ﷺ) said:

> "May his nose be covered with dust, may his nose be covered with dust, may his nose be covered with dust. It was said: 'Who is he, O' Allah's Messenger?' He said: 'It is he whose parents, both or either attain old age while he is alive and is not admitted to Paradise (because of his undutifulness

[3] The Prophet mentioned dutifulness to parents immediately after the act of performing prayers and before Jihad.

[4] Bukhari and Muslim, refer to *Ṣaḥīḥ at-Targhīb wat-Tarhīb.*

to them, and then dies in such a state).' "[5]

2. Anas ibn Mālik (رضي الله عنه) said: "Once the Prophet (ﷺ) ascended the first step of his pulpit and said: '*Āmīn* (so be it with Allah's Will).'" Then he ascended the second step of his pulpit and said: '*Āmīn*. Thereafter he ascended the third step and said: '*Āmīn*. Then he sat on the pulpit. His Companions said: "Why did you say *Āmīn*?" He, (ﷺ) said:

> "Gibrīl (Gabriel) came to me and said: 'May his nose be covered with dust the one before whom your name is mentioned and he does not send prayers on you.' Then I said: '*Āmīn*.' Then he (Gibrīl) said: 'May his nose be covered with dust, the one whose parents attain old age while he is alive and is not admitted to Paradise (because of his undutifulness to them and then dies in such a state).' Then I said: '*Āmīn*.' He then said: 'May his nose be covered with dust, the one who witnesses Ramadan and he is not forgiven (or his sins are not forgiven because he did not make good use of it by performing righteous deeds).' Then I said: '*Āmīn*.' "[6]

3. Jābir ibn Abu Samurah (رضي الله عنه) narrated: "The Prophet (ﷺ) once ascended the pulpit and said: '*Āmīn, Āmīn, Āmīn*.'"

---

[5] Muslim, vol. 8, hadith nos. 5 & 6.

[6] This hadith has been authenticated by al-Albāni in his treatise *Faḍl aṣ-Ṣalāt 'ala an-Nabi* (The Merit of Sending Prayers on the Prophet).

Then he (ﷺ) said:

> "Gibrīl came to me and said: 'O' Muhammad, he whose parents attain old age while he is alive and then dies and enters Hell-fire, then may Allah curse him, say *Āmīn*.' So I said: '*Āmīn*.' Then he said: 'O' Muhammad, whosoever witnesses Ramadan, then he dies and is not forgiven, enters Hell-fire, may Allah curse him, say *Āmīn*.' And I said: '*Āmīn*.' Then he said: 'And before whom you are mentioned and he does not send his prayers on you, and he dies in such a state enters Hell-fire, may Allah curse him, say *Āmīn*.' Thereupon I said: '*Āmīn*.' "[7]

Ibn Ḥibbān narrated that Abu Hurayrah (رضي الله عنه) reported that the Prophet (ﷺ) said:

> "He whose parents, — one or both of them — attain old age while he is alive, and is not dutiful to them, and dies (in such a state) and then enters Hell-fire, may Allah curse him, say *Āmīn* (O' Muhammad)." I then said: '*Āmīn*.' "[8]

Al-Ḥākim and others narrated this hadith in other wordings from Ka'b ibn 'Ajrah — the end of the hadith states:

---

[7] *Ṣaḥīḥ at-Targhīb wat-Tarhīb.*
[8] Ibid.

"When I ascended the third (step of the pulpit), he (Gibrīl) said: 'May he be cursed the one whose parents attain old age — one or both of them — while he is alive and they (parents) did not cause him to enter Paradise (because he was undutiful to them).' So I said: '*Āmīn.*' "[9]

4. Mālik ibn 'Amr al-Qushayri (ﷺ) narrated, "I heard Allah's Messenger (ﷺ) say:

'Whoever manumits a slave, it would be his ransom from Hell-fire, and the one whose parents attain old age while he is alive and is not forgiven (of his sins), may Allah curse and destroy him.' "[10]

5. Ubay ibn Mālik (ﷺ) narrated that the Prophet (ﷺ) said:

"The one whose parents attain old age — one or both of them — while he is alive, and he enters Hell-fire after that (i.e., after his death), may Allah curse and destroy him."[11]

6. 'Abdullāh ibn 'Amr ibn al-'Āṣ (ﷺ) narrated that the Prophet (ﷺ) said:

"Three (kinds of people) for whom Allah has forbidden Paradise are: the drunkard, the undutiful

---

[9] *Ṣaḥīḥ at-Targhīb wat-Tarhīb.*

[10] Ibid.

[11] *Silsilat al-Aḥādīth aṣ-Ṣaḥīḥah.*

to his parents, and the procurer who allows his wife to be a prostitute."[12]

7. 'Abdullāh ibn 'Umar (رضي الله عنه) related: "The Prophet (ﷺ) said:

'Three (kinds of people) who will never enter Paradise, and Allah will never look at them on the Day of Resurrection, and they are: the undutiful to one's parents, the woman who behaves like men and the procurer.'"[13]

8. 'Abdullāh ibn 'Amr ibn al-'Āṣ (رضي الله عنه) said:

"Three (kinds of people) will not enter Paradise (on the Day of Judgement): the one who reminds people of his charities to them, the undutiful to parents and the drunkard."[14]

9. Abu Umāmah (رضي الله عنه) reported that the Prophet (ﷺ) said:

"Three (kinds of people) from whom Allah will never accept repentance nor ransom on the Day of Resurrection: the undutiful (to one's parents), the one who reminds people of his charities to them and the one who denies the Preordainment."[15]

---

[12] *Ṣaḥīḥ at-Targhīb wat-Tarhīb.*

[13] *Ṣaḥīḥ al-Jāmi'*, hadith no. 3058 and *Ḥijāb al-Mar'ah al-Muslimah*, p. 67.

[14] *Ṣaḥīḥ al-Jāmi'*, hadith no. 7553.

[15] Ibid, hadith no. 3060.

10. ‘Abdullāh ibn ‘Amr ibn al-‘Āṣ (ﷺ) narrated: “The Prophet (ﷺ) said:

> ‘Three (kinds of people) at whom Allah will never look on the Day of Resurrection and they are: the undutiful to one’s parents, the woman who behaves like men and the procurer.’ And three (kinds of people) will never enter Paradise: ‘The undutiful to one’s parents, the drunkard and the one who reminds people of his charities.’ ”[16]

11. Abu ad-Dardā’ (ﷺ) said that the Prophet (ﷺ) said:

> “The following kinds of people will never enter Paradise: the undutiful to one’s parents, the drunkard and the one who denies the Preordainment.”[17]

12. Anas ibn Mālik (ﷺ) said that the Prophet (ﷺ) said:

> “Three kinds of people will never enter Paradise: the drunkard, the undutiful to one’s parents and the reminder of charities (or favours).”[18]

13. ‘Abdullāh ibn ‘Amr ibn al-‘Āṣ (ﷺ) narratedd: “The Prophet (ﷺ) said:

---

[16] *Ṣaḥīḥ al-Jāmi‘*, hadith no. 3066, and *Silsilat al-Aḥādīth aṣ-Ṣaḥīḥah*, hadith no. 674.

[17] *Silsilat al-Aḥādīth aṣ-Ṣaḥīḥah*, hadith no. 675.

[18] Ibid, hadith no. 673.

'Three kinds of people will never enter Paradise: the drunkard, the undutiful (to parents) and the reminder of charities.' "[19]

14. 'Amr ibn Murrah al-Juhany (ﷺ) said: "Once a man came to the Prophet (ﷺ) and said:

'O' Messenger of Allah, I bore witness that there is no true god but Allah, and that you are the Messenger of Allah, I performed the five Prayers, paid the poor due out of my money and observed (fasting) Ramadan.' The Prophet said: 'Whosoever dies in such a state [20] will accompany the prophets, the righteous (truthful) and the martyrs on the Day of Resurrection.' Then he, raised his two (fore and middle) fingers and said: 'Unless he is undutiful to his parents.' "[21]

---

[19] Ibid.

[20] That is, to die while believing in the Oneness of Allah sincerely and worshipping Him alone, establishing the Prophet's Sunnah, performing prayers at their fixed times, paying Zakah and fasting Ramadan, one's abode then will be in Paradise with the prophets, the righteous and the martyrs, provided one is dutiful to one's parents and does not harm them a bit. That is, performing the Islamic obligations admits one to Paradise, provided one is dutiful to one's parents, for being undutiful to them nullifies the rewards of the good deeds.

[21] *Ṣaḥīḥ at-Targhīb wat-Tarhīb.*

Allah's Pleasure comes through the parents' pleasure and His Anger comes through their anger

1. 'Abdullāh ibn 'Amr ibn al-'Āṣ (رضي الله عنه) narrated: "The Prophet (ﷺ) said:

> 'The Lord's pleasure is in the parents' pleasure (i.e., the latter causes the former), and the Lord's anger is in the parents' anger.' "[22]

2. 'Abdullāh ibn 'Amr ibn al-'Āṣ (رضي الله عنه) also reported: "The Prophet (ﷺ) said:

> 'Allah's pleasure is in the parents' pleasure (i.e., the latter causes the former), and His anger is in their anger.' "[23]

3. Abu Hurayrah (رضي الله عنه) related: "The Prophet (ﷺ) said:

> 'The Lord's — the All-Glorious, the Almighty — pleasure is in the parents' pleasure, and the Lord's — the All-Glorious, the Almighty — anger is in the parents' anger (i.e., their anger causes Allah's Anger).' "[24]

---

[22] *Ṣaḥīḥ al-Jāmi'*, hadith no. 3500 and *Silsilat al-Aḥādīth aṣ-Ṣaḥīḥah*, hadith no. 516.

[23] *Ṣaḥīḥ al-Jāmi'*, hadith no. 3501.

[24] *Ṣaḥīḥ at-Targhīb wat-Tarhīb*.

Undutifulness to parents is forbidden

1. Allah (ﷻ) says:

﴿... إِمَّا يَبْلُغَنَّ عِندَكَ ٱلْكِبَرَ أَحَدُهُمَآ أَوْ كِلَاهُمَا فَلَا تَقُل لَّهُمَآ أُفٍّ وَلَا تَنْهَرْهُمَا وَقُل لَّهُمَا قَوْلًا كَرِيمًا ﴿٢٣﴾ وَٱخْفِضْ لَهُمَا جَنَاحَ ٱلذُّلِّ مِنَ ٱلرَّحْمَةِ وَقُل رَّبِّ ٱرْحَمْهُمَا كَمَا رَبَّيَانِى صَغِيرًا ﴿٢٤﴾ رَّبُّكُمْ أَعْلَمُ بِمَا فِى نُفُوسِكُمْ إِن تَكُونُوا۟ صَٰلِحِينَ فَإِنَّهُۥ كَانَ لِلْأَوَّٰبِينَ غَفُورًا ﴿٢٥﴾﴾

(سورة الإسراء: ٢٣-٢٥)

﴾... And that you be dutiful to your parents. If one or both of them attain old age in your life, say not to them, "*Uff*" — a word of disrespect, nor shout at them, but address them in terms of honour. And lower unto them the wing of submission and humility through mercy, and say: 'My Lord! Bestow on them your Mercy as they brought me up when I was a youngster.' Your Lord knows best what is in your inner selves. If you are righteous, then, verily, He is Ever Oft-Forgiving to those who turn unto Him again and again in obedience and in repentance.﴿ *(Qur'an 17: 23-25)*

2. In another place, the All-High says:

﴿وَٱلَّذِى قَالَ لِوَٰلِدَيْهِ أُفٍّ لَّكُمَآ أَتَعِدَانِنِىٓ أَنْ أُخْرَجَ وَقَدْ خَلَتِ
ٱلْقُرُونُ مِن قَبْلِى وَهُمَا يَسْتَغِيثَانِ ٱللَّهَ وَيْلَكَ ءَامِنْ إِنَّ وَعْدَ ٱللَّهِ
حَقٌّ فَيَقُولُ مَا هَٰذَآ إِلَّآ أَسَٰطِيرُ ٱلْأَوَّلِينَ ﴿١٧﴾ أُوْلَٰٓئِكَ ٱلَّذِينَ
حَقَّ عَلَيْهِمُ ٱلْقَوْلُ فِىٓ أُمَمٍ قَدْ خَلَتْ مِن قَبْلِهِم مِّنَ ٱلْجِنِّ وَٱلْإِنسِ
إِنَّهُمْ كَانُواْ خَٰسِرِينَ ﴿١٨﴾ وَلِكُلٍّ دَرَجَٰتٌ مِّمَّا عَمِلُواْ وَلِيُوَفِّيَهُمْ
أَعْمَٰلَهُمْ وَهُمْ لَا يُظْلَمُونَ ﴿١٩﴾ وَيَوْمَ يُعْرَضُ ٱلَّذِينَ كَفَرُواْ عَلَى ٱلنَّارِ
أَذْهَبْتُمْ طَيِّبَٰتِكُمْ فِى حَيَاتِكُمُ ٱلدُّنْيَا وَٱسْتَمْتَعْتُم بِهَا فَٱلْيَوْمَ تُجْزَوْنَ
عَذَابَ ٱلْهُونِ بِمَا كُنتُمْ تَسْتَكْبِرُونَ فِى ٱلْأَرْضِ بِغَيْرِ ٱلْحَقِّ وَبِمَا كُنتُمْ
تَفْسُقُونَ ﴿٢٠﴾﴾ (سورة الأحقاف: ١٧-٢٠)

﴾And he who says to his parents: 'Fie upon you both! Do you hold out the promise to me that I shall be raised up [again] when generations before me have passed away [without rising]?' While they [father and mother] invoke Allah for help [and rebuke their son]: 'Woe to you! Believe! Verily, the promise of Allah is true.' But he says: 'This is nothing but the tales of the ancient.' They are those against whom the Word [of torment] is justified among the previous generations of jinn and mankind that have passed away. Verily, they are ever the losers. And for all, there will be degrees according to that which they did, that He [Allah] may recompense them in full for their deeds. And they will not be wronged. On the Day when those who disbelieve [in the Oneness of Allah — Islamic Monotheism] will be exposed to the Fire [it will be said]: 'You received [and abused] your good things in the life of the world, and you took your pleasure therein. Today, you shall be recompensed with a torment of humiliation, because you were arrogant on earth without a right, and because you used to rebel and disobey [Allah].❫ *(Qur'an 46: 17-20)*

3. Al-Mughīrah ibn Shu'bah (رضي الله عنه) reported that the Prophet (ﷺ) said:

"Verily, Allah has forbidden you from being undutiful to mothers,[25] burying girls alive, abstaining (from giving others their rights) and usurping (unjustly the rights of others). And He disapproves of you: irrelevant talk (especially in religious matters for the purpose of exciting disputes among Muslims), persistent questioning, and wasting of wealth (extravagantly)."[26]

4. 'Abdullāh ibn 'Amr ibn al-'Āṣ (رضي الله عنه) related: "The Prophet (ﷺ) said:

'Verily, Allah, the Exalted, Almighty, does not like

---

[25] That is, to be disobedient to them, causing their anger, and not providing subsistence for them, for doing all this is a grave sin that incurs a severe torment on oneself.

[26] Muslim, vol. 5, hadith no. 131.

undutifulness to parents.' "[27]

5. Abu Umāmah (ﷺ) narrated that the Prophet (ﷺ) said:

"Three (kinds of people) from whom Allah will never accept ransom nor repentance on the Day of Resurrection: the undutiful (to one's parents), the boaster of charities (or favours) and that who denies the preordainment."[28]

Undutifulness to parents is a grave sin

1. Abu Bakrah (ﷺ) reported that, "The Prophet (ﷺ) said:

'Should I inform you about the greatest of the great sins?' They said: 'Yes, O' Allah's Messenger.' He said: 'To associate and co-worship others with Allah and to be undutiful to one's parents.' The Prophet then sat (straight) after he had been reclining and said: 'And I warn you against giving a false statement,' and he kept saying that till we wished that he stopped[29] "[30]

---

[27] *Ṣaḥīḥ al-Jāmi'*, hadith no. 1845.

[28] Ibid, hadith no. 3060.

[29] That is: 'We wished that he stopped saying these words out of compassion for him, since we saw signs of anger on his face.'

[30] Bukhari and Muslim, *Ṣaḥīḥ at-Targhīb wat-Tarhīb*.

2. 'Abdullāh ibn 'Amr ibn al-'Āṣ (رضي الله عنه) narrated: "The Prophet (ﷺ) said:

> 'The greatest among the great sins are: associating and co-worshipping partners along with Allah, being undutiful to one's parents and taking a perjury oath[31].'"[32]

3. Anas ibn Mālik (رضي الله عنه) said: "Once great sins were mentioned in the presence of Allah's Messenger, he said:

> 'They are: associating partners along with Allah and being undutiful to (one's) parents.'"[33]

4. The Prophet (ﷺ) once sent a letter with 'Amr ibn Ḥazm to the people of Yemen and wrote in it:

> "Among the greatest of the great sins in Allah's sight on the Day of Resurrection are: associating and co-worshipping partners to Allah, killing a believing soul without a just right, turning one's back in the battle for the cause of Allah, being undutiful to one's parents, slandering the married, righteous and believing women, learning (and dealing with) magic, consuming usury and eating (unjustly) the orphan's property."[34]

---

[31] By which one usurps others' rights.

[32] Bukhari.

[33] Ibid.

[34] Ibn Ḥibbān in his *Ṣaḥīḥ*, refer to *Ṣaḥīḥ at-Targhīb wat-Tarhīb*.

Dutifulness to parents precedes fighting in Allah's cause (Jihad)

1. 'Abdullāh ibn Mas'ūd (🙏) reported: "I asked Allah's Messenger about the best deed." He (🙏) said:

> 'Performing prayers at their fixed times.' I said: 'Then what comes next?' He said: 'Being dutiful to (one's) parents.' [35] I said: 'Then what is next?' He said: 'Fighting in Allah's cause.'"

Leaving Jihad for (the purpose of) serving parents; because Paradise is underneath their feet

1. 'Abdullāh ibn 'Amr ibn al-'Āṣ (🙏) narrated:

> "A man came to the Prophet (🙏) and said: 'I give you the pledge of allegiance that I shall emigrate (from the disbelieving country to the believing one), strive (fight) in Allah's cause, seeking Allah's rewards.' The Prophet said: 'Is any of your parents alive?' The man said: 'Yes, both of them.' He then said: 'And you seek Allah's rewards?' The

---

[35] The Prophet, mentioned dutifulness to parents just after performing prayers, and before Jihad (fighting in Allah's cause).

man replied in the affirmative. He said: '(In that case) return to your parents and be dutiful to them.' "[36]

2. In another hadith, 'Abdullāh ibn 'Amr ibn al-'Āṣ (رضي الله عنه) reported:

"A man came to the Prophet to ask him his permission to participate in Jihad (fighting in Allah's cause)." He said: 'Are your parents alive?' The man replied in the affirmative. Then he said: 'Then exert yourself in their service.' "[37]

3. 'Abdullāh ibn 'Amr ibn al-'Āṣ (رضي الله عنه) related:

"A man came to the Prophet and said: 'I have come to give you the pledge of allegiance to migrate (from the disbelieving country to the believing one), and I had left my parents crying.' The Prophet said: 'Return to them and make them laugh (or pleased) as you had caused them to cry.' "[38]

4. Abu Hurayrah (رضي الله عنه) reported:

"A man came to the Prophet to ask for his permission to participate in Jihad." The Prophet (صلى الله عليه وسلم) said: 'Are your parents alive?' The man

---

[36] Muslim, vol. 8, hadith no. 3.

[37] Bukhari and Muslim, refer to *Ṣaḥīḥ at-Targhīb wat-Tarhīb*.

[38] Abu Dawūd, refer to *Ṣaḥīḥ at-Targhīb wat-Tarhīb*.

replied in the affirmative. He said: 'Then exert yourself in their service.' "[39]

5. Ṭalḥah ibn Mu'āwiyah as-Sulami (ﷺ) narrated:

"I once came to the Prophet and said: 'O' Prophet of Allah I want to fight (or participate in fighting) in Allah's cause.' He (ﷺ) said: 'Is your mother alive?' I said: 'Yes,' He said: 'Lower yourself to her foot,[40] for Paradise is at her feet.' "[41]

6. Mu'āwiyah ibn Jāhimah reported that,

"Jāhimah came to the Prophet and said: 'O' Messenger of Allah, I want to participate in Jihad, and I have come to counsel with you.' He (ﷺ) said: 'Do you have a mother (who is alive)?' I said, 'Yes.' He said: 'Stay near her, for Paradise is underneath her foot[42].' "[43]

7. Mu'āwiyah ibn Jāhimah (ﷺ) related, in another hadith:

---

[39] Muslim and Abu Dawūd, refer to *Ṣaḥīḥ at-Targhīb wat-Tarhīb*.

[40] That is lower yourself in humility, obey her, serve her and be kind to her, and, consequently, you will be admitted to Paradise.

[41] Ṭabrāni, and al-Albāni considered it sound, refer to *Ṣaḥīḥ at-Targhīb wat-Tarhīb*.

[42] This is a metonymy, which indicates granting them honour, pleasing them and acting with humility towards them. Allah says: ﴿And lower to them the wing of humility and show mercy unto them.﴾

[43] Ibn Mājah and Nasā'i, and al-Albāni considered it as authentic, See *Ṣaḥīḥ at-Targhīb wat-Tarhīb*.

"I came to the Prophet to ask for his permission to participate in Jihad." He said: "Do you have parents (who are alive?)" I said: "Yes." He then said: "Stay near them, for underneath their feet lies Paradise."[44]

8. Abu Sa'īd (رضي الله عنه) narrated:

"A man from Yemen emigrated to the Prophet (to stay with him)." He (ﷺ) said: "Do you have any relatives in Yemen?" The man said: "My parents." The Prophet then asked: "Had they given you the permission to emigrate?" The man said: "No." The Prophet then said: "Return to them and ask them for their permission. If they give you their permission (to emigrate and fight along with me in Allah's cause), then fight; otherwise, (stay with them and) treat them kindly (and be dutiful to them)."[45]

---

[44] Ṭabarāni and is authenticated by al-Albāni in *Ṣaḥīḥ at-Targhīb wat-Tarhīb*.

[45] *Ṣaḥīḥ al-Jāmi'*, hadith no. 905 and *Irwā' al-Ghalīl* hadith no. 1199.

Dutifulness to parents is of the righteous deeds one can invoke Allah with

'Abdullāh ibn 'Umar (رضي الله عنه) narrated that the Prophet (ﷺ) said:

> "Once upon a time three men were walking and a heavy rain overtook them. They reached and entered a cave in a mountain for shelter. A big rock rolled down and closed the mouth of the cave. They said to one another: 'Nothing could save you from this rock, but to invoke Allah by giving reference to the righteous deeds which you have done, for Allah's sake only.' So, one of them said: 'O' Allah! I had old parents (whom I used to provide with milk first), and I never provided my family (wife and children) with milk before them. One day, by chance, I was delayed, and I came late (at night) after they had slept. I milked the sheep and took the milk to them, but I found them sleeping. I disliked providing my family with milk before them. So, I waited for them with the bowl of milk in my hand, and I kept waiting for them to get up, till the day dawned. Then, they got up and drank their milk. O' Allah! If I did that for Your sake only, please relieve us from this critical

situation caused by this rock.' So the rock shifted a little, but they could not get out. The Prophet added that the second man said: 'O' Allah! I had a cousin who was the dearest of all people to me, and I wanted to have sexual intercourse with her, but she refused. She later asked for hundred dinars to meet some of her indispensable needs. I then collected hundred dinars and went to her and gave it to her. I then sat on her legs to fulfill my desire, at that moment she said: 'O' Slave of Allah! Fear God and do not break the seal without right, that is, sex is valid only after legitimate marriage.' So, I left her. O' Allah, If I did that for Your sake only, please relieve us from the present calamity.' So, the rock shifted a little more, but still they could not get out of there. The Prophet added that thereafter the third man said: 'O' Allah! I employed few labourers and I paid them their wages with the exception of one man, who did not take his wages and went away. I invested his wages and I got much property thereby. After sometime, he came back and said to me: 'O' Allah's slave! Pay me my wages.' I said to him: 'All the camels, cows, sheep, and slaves you see there, are yours.' He said: 'O' Allah's slave! Don't mock at me.' I said: 'I am not mocking at you.' So he took the entire herd and drove them away and left nothing. O' Allah! If I did that for Your sake only, please relieve us from the present suffering.' So, the rock shifted completely and they got out, walking.' "[46]

Parents' pleasure precedes the wife's pleasure

1. Ibn 'Umar (ﷺ) said:

"I married a woman whom I loved much, but 'Umar (his father) hated her and commanded me to divorce her, but I refused. Then he went to the Prophet (ﷺ) and told him the matter." The Prophet said to me: "Divorce her."[47]

2. Abu ad-Dardā' (ﷺ) narrated:

"Once a man came to me and said: 'I have a wife whom my mother asks me to divorce.' I said: 'I heard the Messenger of Allah (ﷺ) say: 'The parents are the middle door among the doors of Paradise[48]; you can lose it or win it, if you so wish.' ' "[49]

---

[46] Bukhari and Muslim, refer to *Ṣaḥīḥ at-Targhīb wat-Tarhīb*. And *Ṣaḥīḥ al-Jāmi'*, hadith no. 2867.

[47] *Ṣaḥīḥ at-Targhīb wat-Tarhīb.*

[48] The middle door means the best door of Paradise. (That is, being dutiful to parents leads one to enter Paradise through its best door). (Translator)

[49] *Ṣaḥīḥ at-Targhīb wat-Tarhīb.*

3. Ibn Ḥibbān (ﷺ) narrated the previous hadith in another wordings in his *Ṣaḥīḥ*:

> "A man came to Abu ad-Dardā' and said: 'My father kept asking me to get married, till I did, and now he orders me to divorce my wife.' " Abu ad-Dardā' said: "I will neither advise you to be undutiful to your parents, nor will I command you to divorce your wife. But I will tell you something I heard from the Prophet (ﷺ). I heard the Prophet say: 'The parents are the middle door of Paradise; you could either lose it or win it.' "[50]

4. Mu'ādh ibn Jabal (ﷺ) said: "The Messenger of Allah enjoined on me to do ten things." He (ﷺ) said:

> "Do not associate anything with Allah, even if you are killed or burnt, and do not be undutiful to your parents even if they command you to abandon your beloved ones and your property."[51]

Dutifulness to mother precedes dutifulness to father

1. Abu Hurayrah (ﷺ) narrated: "A man came to Allah's Messenger and said: 'O' Allah's Messenger! Who is more

---

[50] *Ṣaḥīḥ at-Targhīb wat-Tarhīb.*

[51] Ibid.

entitled to be treated with my best companionship?' The Prophet (ﷺ) said:

> 'Your mother.' The man said: 'Who is next?' He said: 'Your mother.' The man then said: 'Who is next?' He said: 'Your mother.' The man then said: 'Who is next?' He said: 'Your father.' "[52]

2. Abu Hurayrah (ﷺ) narrated that the Prophet (ﷺ) said:

> "Be dutiful and kind to your mother, then your mother, then your mother, then your father, then those who are lower in the rank of kinship, then the lowest."[53]

3. In another hadith, the Prophet (ﷺ) said:

> "Be dutiful and kind to your mother, your father, your sister, your brother, then the lower in kinship, then the lowest."[54]

4. Al-Miqdām (ﷺ) reported that the Prophet (ﷺ) said:

---

[52] This hadith indicates that the mother has a right which equals three folds that of the father, and this is due to the hardship the mother faces during pregnancy, delivery, and fostering the child. Then after birth, the father shares her the responsibility of raising the child. This is mentioned also in the Holy Qur'an as: ﴾And We have enjoined on man [to be dutiful and good] to his parents. His mother bore him in weakness upon weakness, and his weaning is in two years.﴿ (Qur'an 31: 14)

[53] *Ṣaḥīḥ al-Jami'*, hadith no. 1395.

[54] Ibid, hadith no. 1396.

"Verily, Allah enjoins on you to be dutiful to your mother (thrice), and Allah, the Almighty, enjoins on you to be dutiful to your father (twice), and Allah, the All-High, enjoins on you to be dutiful and kind to the nearest in kinship then the nearer."[55]

Parents' invocations are answerable

1. Abu Hurayrah (رضي الله عنه) related that the Prophet (ﷺ) said:

   "Three (kinds of) invocations are certainly answered: the invocation of the parent for or against his son (or daughter), the invocation of the traveller and the invocation of the oppressed."[56]

2. Anas ibn Mālik (رضي الله عنه) reported that the Prophet (ﷺ) said:

   "Three (kinds of) invocations are not turned down: the invocation of the parent for his son (or daughter), the invocation of the one observing *Ṣawm* (fasting), and the invocation of the traveller."[57]

3. Abu Hurayrah (رضي الله عنه) narrated that the Prophet (ﷺ) said:

   "Three invocations are undoubtedly answered: the

---

[55] *Ṣaḥīḥ al-Jami'*, hadith no. 1920.

[56] Ibid, hadith no. 3028.

[57] Ibid, hadith no. 3029.

invocation of the oppressed, the invocation of the traveller and the invocation of the parent for his son (or daughter)."[58]

Kindness to parents

Dutifulness to parents include:

1. Appropriate kindness to them,
2. Invoking Allah's blessings for them,
3. Paying attention to their advises (in this world) and,
4. Craving after their guidance to the right path even if they be non-Muslims.

1. Allah (ﷻ) says:

﴿وَإِن جَٰهَدَاكَ عَلَىٰٓ أَن تُشْرِكَ بِى مَا لَيْسَ لَكَ بِهِۦ عِلْمٌ فَلَا تُطِعْهُمَا ۖ وَصَاحِبْهُمَا فِى ٱلدُّنْيَا مَعْرُوفًا ۖ وَٱتَّبِعْ سَبِيلَ مَنْ أَنَابَ إِلَىَّ ۚ ثُمَّ إِلَىَّ مَرْجِعُكُمْ فَأُنَبِّئُكُم بِمَا كُنتُمْ تَعْمَلُونَ ﴿١٥﴾﴾

(سورة لقمان: ١٥)

﴿But if they endeavour to make you associate with Me, that of which you have no knowledge; then obey them not; but behave kindly with them in the world, and follow the path of him who turns to Me in repentance and obedience. Then to Me will be

---

[58] *Ṣaḥīḥ al-Jami'*, hadith no. 3030.

your return, and I shall tell you what you used to do.﴿ *(Qur'an 31: 15)*

2. Allah (ﷻ) says about Prophet Ibrāhīm (Abraham) (ﷺ):

﴿وَٱذْكُرْ فِى ٱلْكِتَـٰبِ إِبْرَٰهِيمَ ۚ إِنَّهُۥ كَانَ صِدِّيقًا نَّبِيًّا ﴿٤١﴾ إِذْ قَالَ لِأَبِيهِ يَـٰٓأَبَتِ لِمَ تَعْبُدُ مَا لَا يَسْمَعُ وَلَا يُبْصِرُ وَلَا يُغْنِى عَنكَ شَيْـًٔا ﴿٤٢﴾ يَـٰٓأَبَتِ إِنِّى قَدْ جَآءَنِى مِنَ ٱلْعِلْمِ مَا لَمْ يَأْتِكَ فَٱتَّبِعْنِىٓ أَهْدِكَ صِرَٰطًا سَوِيًّا ﴿٤٣﴾ يَـٰٓأَبَتِ لَا تَعْبُدِ ٱلشَّيْطَـٰنَ ۖ إِنَّ ٱلشَّيْطَـٰنَ كَانَ لِلرَّحْمَـٰنِ عَصِيًّا ﴿٤٤﴾ يَـٰٓأَبَتِ إِنِّىٓ أَخَافُ أَن يَمَسَّكَ عَذَابٌ مِّنَ ٱلرَّحْمَـٰنِ فَتَكُونَ لِلشَّيْطَـٰنِ وَلِيًّا ﴿٤٥﴾﴾ (سورة مريم: ٤١-٤٥)

﴾And mention in the Book [the story of] Ibrāhīm [Abraham]. Verily, he was a man of truth, a prophet. When he said to his father: 'O' my father! Why do you worship that which hears not, sees not and can not avail you in anything? O' my father! Verily, there has come to me of the knowledge, that which came not to you. So follow me, I will guide you to the Straight Path. O' my father! Worship not the *Shayṭān* [Satan]. Verily, *Shayṭān* has ever been a rebel against the Most Beneficent [Allah]. O' my father! Verily I fear lest a torment from the Most Beneficent [Allah] should overtake you, so that you become a companion of *Shayṭān* [in Hell-fire].﴿ *(Qur'an 19: 41-45)*

3. Allah (ﷻ) says:

﴿ يَـٰٓأَيُّهَا ٱلَّذِينَ ءَامَنُوا۟ كُونُوا۟ قَوَّٰمِينَ بِٱلْقِسْطِ شُهَدَآءَ لِلَّهِ وَلَوْ عَلَىٰٓ أَنفُسِكُمْ أَوِ ٱلْوَٰلِدَيْنِ وَٱلْأَقْرَبِينَ ... ﴿١٣٥﴾ ﴾

(سورة النِّساء: ١٣٥)

﴿O', you who believe! Stand out firmly for justice, as witnesses to Allah, even though it be against yourselves, or your parents, or your kin,...﴾

(Qur'an 4: 135)

The above-stated verses indicate that there should be a place of honour in the son's heart towards his parents; that the first he advises, guides to the right path and directs, are those who are nearest [of kin] to him: his parents then his kith and kin, for guiding parents and directing them to Allah's path is of dutifulness to them.

4. Asmā' bint Abi Bakr (رضي الله عنها) 'may Allah be pleased with her', said:

> "My mother came to me during the life time of Allah's Messenger (ﷺ) and she was a *mushrikah* (polytheist) yet. I said to Allah's Messenger — seeking his verdict — 'My mother has come to me and she desires to receive a reward from me, shall I grant her what she wanted and be kind towards her?'" The Prophet (ﷺ) said: "Yes, keep good relation with her."[59]

---

[59] Bukhari, See *Ṣaḥīḥ at-Targhīb wat-Tarhīb*.

5. In another hadith Asma' bint Abi Bakr (رضي الله عنها) said:

"My mother came to me recently and she desired to receive a reward from me, and she was a *mushrikah* and she severely detested Islam." I said: "O' Messenger of Allah, my mother came to me and she detests Islam severely, she is a *mushrikah*, shall I keep good relations with her?" The Prophet (ﷺ) said: "Yes. Keep good relation with her."[60]

6. Abu Hurayrah (رضي الله عنه) said:

"I always used to call my mother to embrace Islam when she was a *mushrikah*. One day, I tried to call her to embrace Islàm, but she (instead) abused Allah's Messenger. Thereafter, I came to the Messenger of Allah (ﷺ) with my eyes shedding tears." I said: "O' Allah's Messenger, I used to call my mother to Islam and she used to refuse. Today, I called her (to Islam) and she talked obscenely about you, so, please pray to Allah to guide her to Islam. The Prophet said: "O' Allah, guide Abu Hurayrah's mother (to Islam). Hearing that, I went out seeing good omen in the Prophet's invocation. When I reached the door (of my house), I found it closed. My mother heard the creaking of my feet,

---

[60] Abu Dawūd, See *Ṣaḥīḥ at-Targhīb wat-Tarhīb*.

> thereupon she said: 'Stay where you are, Abu Hurayrah.' I could hear the jogging of water (she was taking a bath). He (Abu Hurayrah) said: 'She bathed, then wore her mantle, but was so much in a hurry to wear her head veil, and quickly opened the door and said: 'O' Abu Hurayrah, I bear witness that there in no god but Allah, and I bear witness that Muhammad is His Slave and Messenger.'''"

Abu Hurayrah said: "I returned joyfully to Allah's Messenger (ﷺ) and my eyes shedding tears and said: 'O' Messenger of Allah, hear the glad tidings, Allah has just granted you your invocation, and guided Abu Hurayrah's mother (to Islam).'" The Prophet (ﷺ) praised Allah and said nice words (on this occasion). I (Abu Hurayrah) then said: "O' Messenger of Allah, invoke Allah that believing people love my mother, and me and that we love them. The Prophet (ﷺ) then said:

> 'O' Allah let the believing slaves (Muslims) love this bondman (Abu Hurayrah) and his mother, and make them love the believing people. Thereafter, no Muslim ever hears about me or sees me but likes me.'"[61]

7. Muṣ'ab ibn Sa'd (رضي الله عنه) narrated from his father (Sa'd ibn Abi Waqqaṣ) saying that some verses of the Holy Qur'an

[61] Muslim, vol. 7 hadith no. 165.

concerning him were revealed. He (Sa'd) said: "Sa'd's mother swore that she would never talk to him till he disbelieves in his religion, and she would never eat or drink." She said: "You claim that Allah has enjoined on you to be dutiful to your parents, and I am your mother, and I command you to do this (i.e., disbelieve in Islam). She remained in that state (i.e., not eating nor drinking) for three days, till she fainted out of exhaustion: A son of hers named 'Umārah provided her with water (then she drank), then she invoked for Allah's curse against Sa'd. Thereupon, Allah (ﷻ) revealed the following verses:

﴿وَوَصَّيْنَا ٱلْإِنسَـٰنَ بِوَٰلِدَيْهِ حُسْنًا ... ﴿٨﴾﴾ (سورة العنكبوت: ٨)

﴿And We have enjoined upon man goodness to parents...﴾ *(Qur'an 29: 8)*

﴿... وَإِن جَـٰهَدَاكَ عَلَىٰٓ أَن تُشْرِكَ بِى مَا لَيْسَ لَكَ بِهِۦ عِلْمٌ فَلَا تُطِعْهُمَا ۖ وَصَاحِبْهُمَا فِى ٱلدُّنْيَا مَعْرُوفًا ... ﴿١٥﴾﴾

(سورة لقمان: ١٥)

﴿But if they endeavour to make you associate with Me, that of which you have no knowledge, then obey them not, but behave kindly with them in the world.﴾ *(Qur'an 31: 15)* [62]

[62] Muslim, vol. 7, hadith nos. 125 & 126.

The Parents' favour to their children is great

Abu Hurayrah (رضي الله عنه) narrated that the Prophet (ﷺ) said:

> "A son (or daughter) would never recompense his/her) parent's favour except when he or she (the son or the daughter) finds him/her (the parent) a slave, buys him/her, then manumits him/her)."[63]

Abusing and cursing one's parents is a great sin

1. 'Abdullāh ibn 'Amr ibn al-'Āṣ (رضي الله عنهما) related: The Prophet (ﷺ) said:

> "It is of the greatest sins that a man curses his parents. It was asked: 'O' Allah's Messenger! How does a man curse his (own) parents?' He said: 'The man abuses the father of another man, and then the latter abuses the father of the former, and abuses his mother, and then the latter abuses the former's mother.' "[64]

2. In another hadith it is reported:

---

[63] Muslim, vol. 4, hadith no. 218. *Ṣaḥīḥ al-Jami'*, hadith no. 7498.

[64] Bukhari, Muslim, and Abu Dawūd. See *Ṣaḥīḥ at-Targhīb wat-Tarhīb*.

"It is of the greatest sins that a man curses his parents." It was asked: "O' Allah's Messenger! How does a man curse his parents?" He (ﷺ) said: "A man curses another man's father, and the latter curses his father or he curses another man's mother, and the latter curses his mother."[65]

3. 'Āmir ibn Wāthilah (رضي الله عنه) narrated: "I had been with 'Ali ibn Abi Ṭālib (رضي الله عنه) when a man came to him and said: 'What had the Prophet (ﷺ) told you secretly (before he died)?'" He ('Ali) got angry and said: "The Prophet had never told me anything secretly, to the exclusion of other people, but he had only told me four words (things)." The man said: "What are they, O' Commander of the believers?" He said that the Prophet (ﷺ) said:

"May Allah curse him, he who curses his parents. May Allah curse him, the one who slaughters (as a sacrifice) for other than Allah. May Allah curse him, who protects and supports an innovator in religion. And may Allah curse him, who changes the marks (that show the boundaries) of lands (in order to usurp the properties of other people)."[66] [These acts were done by the people of the Days of ignorance (pre-Islamic era), who were polytheists.]

---

[65] Bukhari and Muslim. See *Ṣaḥīḥ at-Targhīb wat-Tarhīb.*

[66] Muslim, vol. 6, hadith no. 84.

4. Ibn 'Abbās (رضي الله عنه) related that the Prophet (ﷺ) said:

> "Accursed is he who abuses his father. Accursed is he who abuses his mother. Accursed is he who slaughters (as a sacrifice) for other than Allah. Accursed is he who changes the marks (or boundaries) of lands (to usurp others' lands unjustly). Accursed is he who misleads a blind person. Accursed is he who has sexual intercourse with a beast, and cursed is he who follows the act of the people of Lūṭ (Lot) (عليه السلام) (i.e., sodomy)."[67]

The son is of his father's earnings

1. Jābir ibn 'Abdullāh (رضي الله عنه) narrated that a man came to the Prophet (ﷺ) and said:

> "I have money and children, and my father wants to take my money by force. The Prophet said: 'You and your money are for (or under service of) your father.'"

2. 'Abdullāh ibn 'Amr ibn al-'Āṣ (رضي الله عنه) reported:

> "Once a nomad came to the Prophet and said: 'I own money and I have children, and my father wants to take my money (i.e., take it all).'" He (ﷺ)

---

[67] *Ṣaḥīḥ al-Jāmi'*, hadith no. 5767.

said: "You and your money are for your father (i.e., under his service). Your children are the best of your earnings, so eat and benefit from your children's earnings."[68]

3. 'Ā'ishah, (رضي الله عنها) related that the Prophet (ﷺ) said:

"The best of that from which you could eat is that which you earned yourselves, and your sons are of your earnings."[69]

4. 'Ā'ishah, (رضي الله عنها), narrated in another hadith:

The best of that from which man could eat and benefit is from his earnings, and his son is (considered) of his earnings.[70]

5. Yet in another hadith she (رضي الله عنها) said [from the Prophet (ﷺ)]:

"The man's son is of his earnings, the best of his earnings, so eat of their money or properties (i.e., get benefit from them)."[71]

6. 'Abdullāh ibn 'Umar (رضي الله عنهما) reported:

"A man came to the Prophet and said: 'O' Allah's

---

[68] *Irwā' al-Ghalīl*, hadith no. 838; *Ṣaḥīḥ al-Jami'*, hadith no. 1499.

[69] Ibid, hadith no. 1626; *Ṣaḥīḥ al-Jami'*, hadith no. 1562.

[70] Ibid, hadith no. 838.

[71] *Ṣaḥīḥ al-Jami'*, hadith no. 6996.

Messenger! My father took my money.'" The Prophet (ﷺ) gave him a credit, "You and your money are properties of your father."[72]

7. In another report, Ibn 'Umar (رضي الله عنه) related that the Prophet (ﷺ) said:

"The son (off-spring) is of the father's earnings."[73]

8. 'Abdullāh ibn 'Umar (رضي الله عنه) narrated:

"A man came to the Prophet, complaining against his father saying: 'He took my money.'" The Prophet said: "Have you been informed that you and your money are of your father's earnings?"[74]

Dutifulness to parents after their death

1. 'Abdullāh ibn 'Umar (رضي الله عنه) had a donkey. When he would leave for Makkah, he would change his ride to the donkey when he was tired of riding the camel. He had a turban which he used to wear on his head. One day, while he was riding his donkey, a nomad came across him. 'Abdullāh said: "Are you not the son of so and so?" The nomad said:

---

[72] *Irwạ' al-Ghalīl*, hadith no. 838.

[73] Ibid, hadith no. 838; *Ṣaḥiḥ al-Jami'*, hadith no. 7039.

[74] *Silsilat al-Aḥādīth aṣ-Ṣaḥīḥah*, hadith no. 1548.

"Yes, I am." 'Abdullāh thereafter gave him the donkey and said, "Ride this," and gave him the turban and said, "Wrap your head with it." Some of his companions said to him: "May Allah forgive you, you gave this nomad the donkey which you used to ride when you felt tired of riding the camel, and the turban with which you used to wrap your head?" 'Abdullāh said: "I heard Allah's Messenger (ﷺ) say:

> 'It is one of the most righteous deeds that a man should keep good relations with his father's friends and beloved ones after his death. The nomad's father was a friend for 'Umar (i.e., my father).' "[75]

2. Abu Bardah stated: "I came to Madīnah, then 'Abdullāh ibn 'Umar came to me and said: 'Do you know why I have come to you.' Abu Bardah replied: 'No.' Then, he said: 'Whoever wants to keep good relations with his father, though he is in the grave, should keep good relation with his father's friends after his death. And my father ('Umar) and your father used to be good friends, and I wanted to keep that relation.' "[76]

3. 'Abdullāh ibn 'Umar narrated that the Prophet (ﷺ) said:

> "It is of righteousness to keep good relation with your father's friends."[77]

---

[75] Muslim, vol. 8, hadith no. 6.

[76] *Ṣaḥīḥ at-Targhīb wat-Tarhīb.*

[77] *Ṣaḥīḥ al-Jāmi'*, hadith no. 5777.

Parents should raise their children well to make them righteous

Abu Hurayrah (رضي الله عنه) narrated that the Prophet (ﷺ) said:

> "When a man dies, his acts come to an end, with the exception of three: 'A recurring charity, knowledge from which people get benefited, and a pious son[78] who prays for him.' "[79]

2. Abu Qatādah (رضي الله عنه) related that the Messenger of Allah (ﷺ) said:

> "The best three things a man could leave after his death are: 'A pious son who would pray for him (asks for Allah's forgiveness for him), a recurring charity the reward of which would go to him (i.e. the deceased) and knowledge by which people get benefited.' "[80]

3. Abu Hurayrah (رضي الله عنه) reported that the Messenger of Allah (ﷺ) said:

> "Verily, the acts of which rewards follow the believer after his death are: 'Knowledge, which he

---

[78] The Prophet said: 'Pious because rewards would not be gained through an evil son.'

[79] Muslim, vol. 5, hadith no. 73, *Aḥkām al-Janā'iz*, p. 176.

[80] Ibn Mājah and others, refer to *Aḥkām al-Janā'iz*, p. 176.

taught and spread (among people), a pious son he left behind (alive to pray for him), a Holy Qur'an which he left as inheritance, a mosque which he built, a house for the wayfarer which he built, a canal he dug for water to flow through or a charity which he gave out of his wealth while healthy and alive, all these (by reward) follow him after his death.' "[81]

4. Ibn 'Abbās (ﷺ) reported that Sa'd ibn Ubādah (ﷺ) came to ask for Allah's Messenger's verdict. He (Sa'd) said:

"My mother died before fulfilling a vow she made in her life, (what should I do?)." He (ﷺ) said: "You should fulfill it on her behalf."[82]

5. Ibn 'Abbās (ﷺ) stated:

'A woman went on a journey by sea, and she made a vow that if Allah (ﷻ) saved her, she would observe fasting for a whole month. However, she did not fast till she died. A relative woman of hers (may be her sister or daughter) came to the Prophet (ﷺ) and told him the whole story. He (ﷺ) said: "What do you say if she was indebted, would you pay back her debt?" The woman said: "Yes." He said: "Allah's debts have more right to be repaid;

---

[81] Ibn Mājah and others, *Aḥkām al-Janā'iz*, p. 176.
[82] Bukhari and Muslim and others. Refer to *Aḥkām al-Janā'iz*, p. 170.

Observe *Ṣawm* (fasting) on your mother's behalf."[83]

6. 'Ā'ishah, (رضي الله عنها) narrated:

   "A man came to the Prophet (ﷺ) and said: 'My mother died suddenly and she had not had the power to write her will, and I think that if she had the power to talk, she would have given charities (of her money). Would there be any reward for her and me if I give out charities on her behalf?' " He replied: "Yes. Give out charities on her behalf."[84]

7. Ibn 'Abbās (رضي الله عنه) reported:

   Sa'd ibn 'Ubādah's mother died while he was travelling away. He (Sa'd) said: "O' Allah's Messenger! My mother died while I was away, would it benefit her if I give out charities on her behalf?" He (ﷺ) said: "Yes." He (Sa'd) then said: "Then bear witness that I have given the fruitful orchard (which she left behind) as a charity on her behalf."[85]

8. Abu Hurayrah (رضي الله عنه) related:

   "A man came to the Prophet and said: 'My father

---

[83] Abu Dawūd and others. See *Aḥkām al-Janạ'iz*, p. 169.

[84] Bukhari and Muslim and others, See *Aḥkām al-Janạ'iz*, p. 172.

[85] Bukhari and others. *Aḥkām al-Janạ'iz*, p. 172.

died and left some money behind, and he had not written a will, would it expiate that I give charities out on his behalf?' The Prophet said: 'Yes.'"[86]

9. Buraydah (رضي الله عنه) narrated:

"Once, I was sitting with the Prophet (ﷺ) when a woman came and said: 'I have given my mother a slave-girl of mine, as a charity, then she (my mother) died. What about the slave girl?' He (ﷺ) said: 'You shall take your reward (for your charity) and you shall get her (the slave girl) back, because of the inheritance (law).' She said: 'O' Allah's Messenger, she died and she ought to have observed *Ṣawm* (fasting) for one month, shall I observe *Ṣawm* on her behalf?' He said: 'Yes, fast on her behalf.' She said: 'She never performed Ḥajj, can I perform Ḥajj on her behalf?' He said: 'Yes. Perform Ḥajj on her behalf.'"[87]

10. Abu Hurayrah (رضي الله عنه) reported that the Prophet (ﷺ) said:

"A person's rank would be elevated in Paradise, and he would say: 'Why was I offered this honour?' It would be said (to him): 'This is due to your son's invocations for forgiveness for you.'"[88]

---

[86] Muslim and others. *Aḥkām al-Janạ'iz*, p. 172.
[87] Muslim, vol. 3, hadith no. 156.
[88] *Ṣaḥīḥ al-Jāmi'*, hadith no. 1613.

Conclusion

Finally, dear Muslim brother and sister, you now know many of the Qur'anic verses that speak of the obligations of being dutiful to one's parents, and treating them kindly, and the verses that describe the Prophets' kindness towards their parents and how they invoked Allah (ﷻ) for their good. And you know now, through the Qur'anic verses and the hadiths, that dutifulness to parents is always joined with worshipping Allah (ﷻ). Dutifulness to parents admits one to Paradise, for Allah's pleasure comes from parents' pleasure, and Allah's anger comes from parents' anger. Besides, undutifulness to parents is forbidden as stated in the Qur'an and the Prophet's Sunnah.

Undutifulness to parents is also considered one of the greatest sins against which Allah's Messenger (ﷺ) warned us. Being kind to them admits us to Paradise by Allah's Will, for Paradise lies under their feet.

We also knew that Parents' invocations are certainly answered, and the parents' favour is very great on us. The Prophet (ﷺ), forbade us from cursing or abusing our parents, and this is done by abstaining from abusing or cursing others' parents. The Prophet (ﷺ) affirmed that we are of our parents' earnings, and that we, ourselves, belong to them, as well as our properties. The Prophet (ﷺ) also commanded us to be dutiful to our parents after their death, and that is done by keeping good relation with their beloved ones.

From all these, dear Muslim brother and sister, we learned from the Qur'anic verses and the Prophetic hadiths, that dutifulness to parents is of paramount importance. Though even one verse commanding us to be dutiful to our parents, would suffice us and urge us to do so. How is the case then, when there are many verses and Prophetic hadiths concerning this matter?

You should, dear Muslim brother and sister, be dutiful to your parents and behave towards them as Allah (ﷻ) and the Prophet (ﷺ), enjoined on you; i.e., to behave well, giving them their rights, so that you could gain happiness in this world and in the Hereafter. Allah (ﷻ) says:

﴿وَمِنْهُم مَّن يَقُولُ رَبَّنَآ ءَاتِنَا فِى ٱلدُّنْيَا حَسَنَةً وَفِى ٱلْـَٔاخِرَةِ حَسَنَةً وَقِنَا عَذَابَ ٱلنَّارِ ﴿٢٠١﴾﴾

(سورة البَقَرَة: ٢٠١)

﴾And there are men who say, 'Our Lord! Give us in this world that which is good and in the Hereafter that which is good and save us from the Torment of Fire.﴿ *(Qur'an 2: 201)*

The last of our invocations is praise be to Allah (ﷻ), the Lord of the world (mankind, jinn, and all that exists).

Symbols' used in this Book

(سبحانه وتعالى) : *Subḥānahu wa Ta'āla* — 'The Exalted'

(ﷺ): *Ṣallā-Allāhu 'Alayhi wa Sallam* — 'Blessings and Peace be upon him'

(عليه السلام): *'Alayhis-Salām* — 'May peace be upon him'

(رضي الله عنه): *Raḍia Allāhu 'Anhū* — 'May Allah be pleased with him'

(رضي الله عنها): *Raḍia Allāhu 'Anhā* — 'May Allah be pleased with her'

Glossary

'Ālamīn	عالمين	: Lit. Worlds, Universe; Mankind, Jinn and all that exists.
Alif-Lām-Mīm	الم	: Abbreviated letters, the *Muqaṭṭa'āt*, the exact meaning is known to Allah alone
D͟hālimūn	ظالِمون	: Sing. *D͟halim*; Polytheists, wrong doers, and disbelievers
Ḥukm	حكم	: Lit. Command, authority; Religious knowledge, right judgement, ruling
Inshā' Allah	إنشاء الله	: If Allah Wills, Allah Willing
Jihad	جِهاد	: Lit. Struggle, striving; Fighting in Allah's Cause
Khaṭīb	خطيب	: The one who delivers sermons
Masākīn	مساكين	: Sing. *Miskīn*; The poor

Muḥsinūn	محسنون	:	Sing. *Muḥsin*; Good doers, pious believers
Mushrikūn	مُشرِكون	:	Sing. *Mushrik*; Polythiests
Nifāq	نِفاق	:	Hypocrisy
Ṣābirīn	صابِرين	:	Sing. *Ṣābir*; The patient ones
Ṣalāh	صلاة / صلوٰة	:	Prayer
Salām	سلام	:	Peace
Ṣawm	صوم	:	Fasting
Zakah	زكوٰة / زكاة	:	Poor-due, a pillar of Islam

Transliteration Chart

أ	a
آ . ى	ā / aa
ب	b
ت	t
ة	h or t (when followed by another Arabic word)
ث	th
ج	j
ح	ḥ
خ	kh
د	d
ذ	dh
ر	r
ز	z
س	s
ش	sh

ص	ṣ
ض	ḍ
ط	ṭ
ظ	dh
ع	‘
غ	gh
ف	f
ق	q
ك	k
ل	l
م	m
ن	n
هـ – ه – ـه	h
و	w
و (as a long vowel)	ū / oo
ي	y
ي (as a long vowel)	ī / ee
ء	’ (Omitted in initial position)